STAR TREK

PIANO SOLO

MUSIC FROM THE MOTION PICTURE

ISBN 978-1-4234-8375-5

HAL•LEONARD®
CORPORATION

7777 W. BLUEMOUND RD. P.O. BOX 13819 MILWAUKEE, WI 53213

In Australia Contact:
Hal Leonard Australia Pty. Ltd.
4 Lentara Court
Cheltenham, Victoria, 3192 Australia
Email: ausadmin@halleonard.com.au

Visit Hal Leonard Online at
www.halleonard.com

CONTENTS

STAR TREK

By MICHAEL GIACCHINO

Moderately slow, in 2

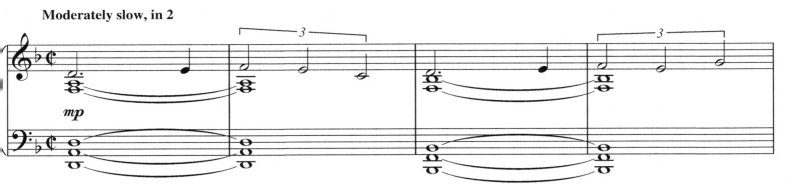

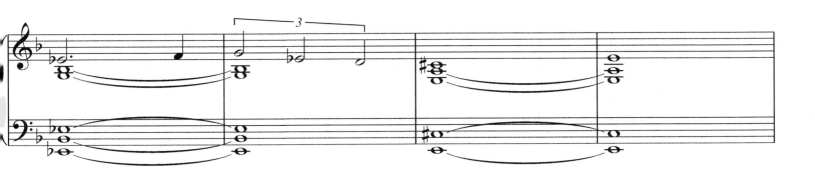

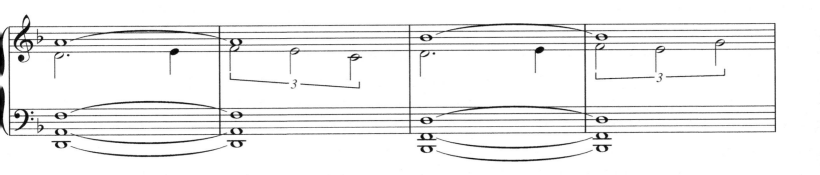

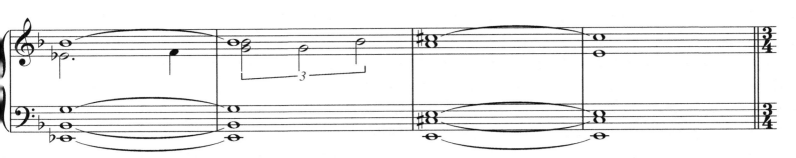

Faster

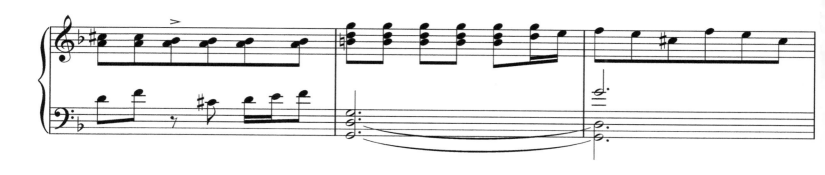

cresc.

LABOR OF LOVE

By MICHAEL GIACCHINO

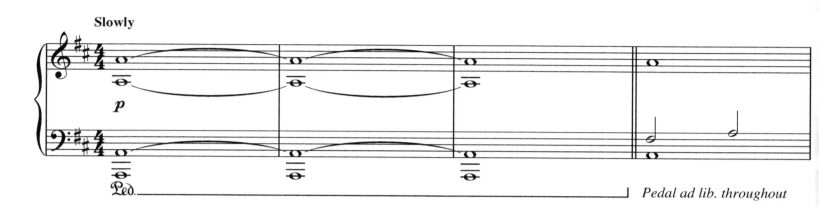

HELLA BAR TALK

By MICHAEL GIACCHINO

Moderately slow

mp

Pedal ad lib. throughout

NICE TO MELD YOU

By MICHAEL GIACCHINO

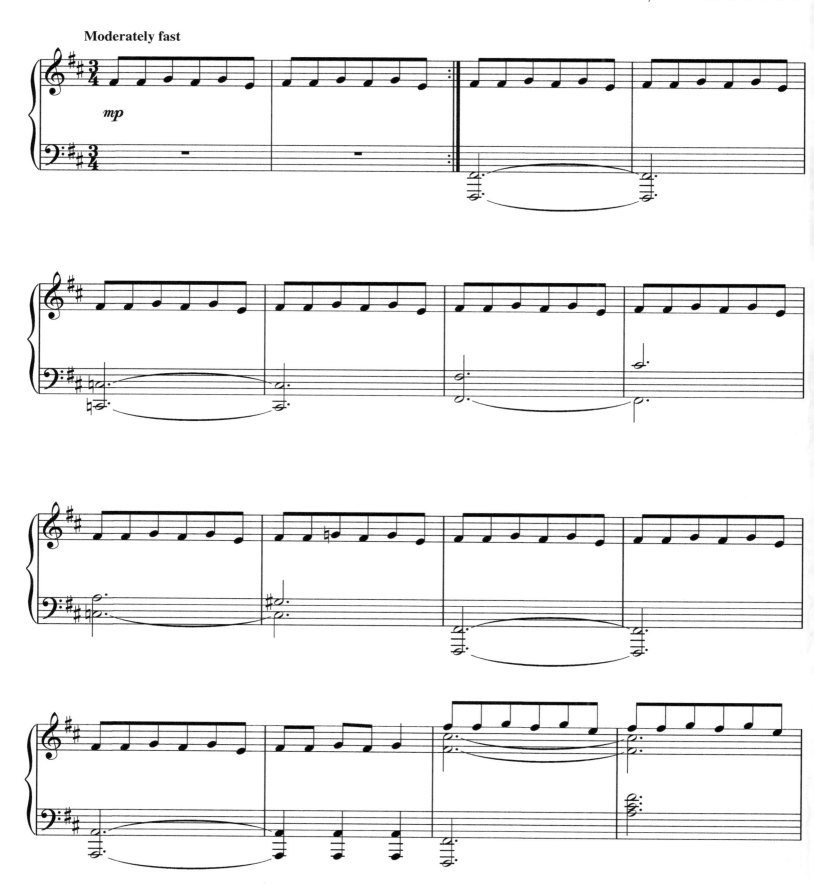

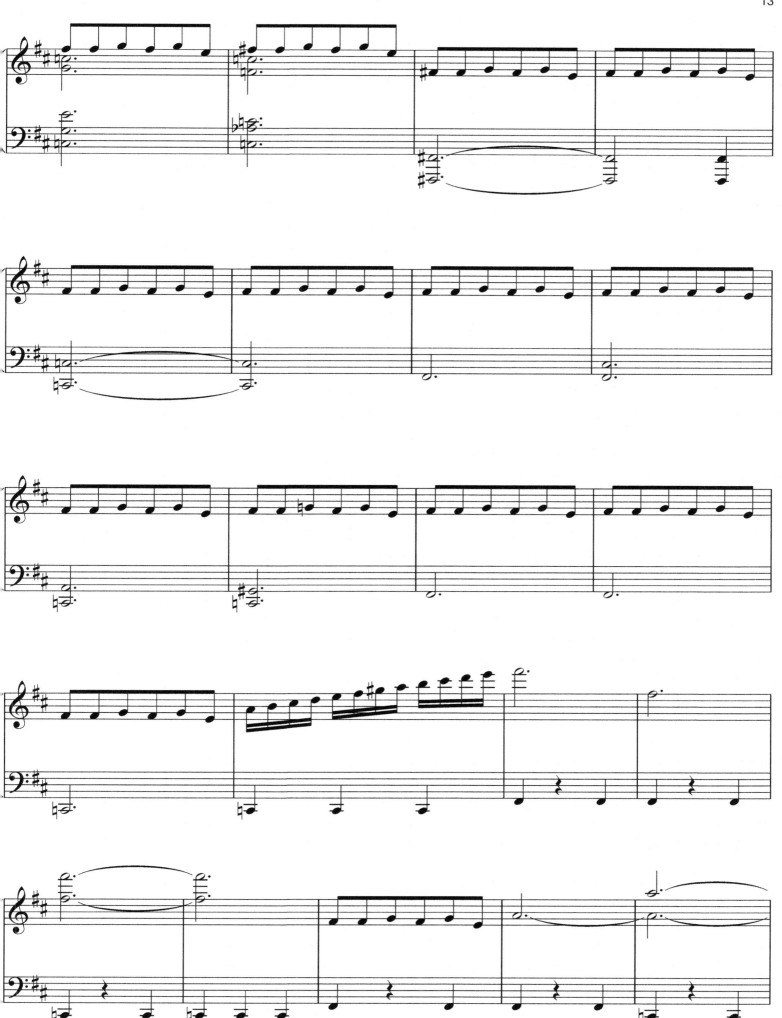

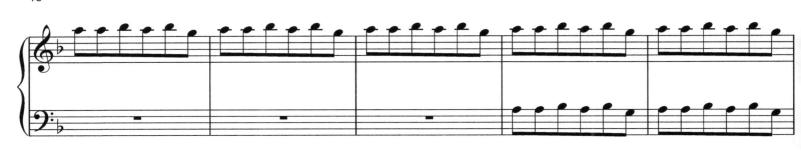

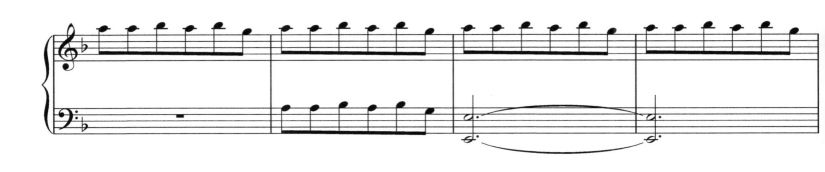

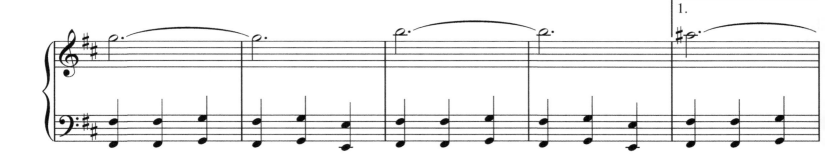

DOES IT STILL McFLY?

By MICHAEL GIACCHINO

NERO FIDDLES, NARADA BURNS

By MICHAEL GIACCHINO

Moderately, in 2

BACK FROM BLACK

By MICHAEL GIACCHINO

THAT NEW CAR SMELL

By MICHAEL GIACCHINO

Moderately slow

Pedal ad lib. throughout

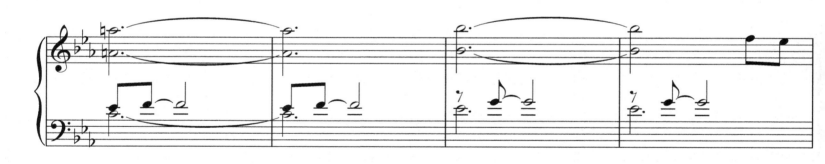

Twice as fast

($\bullet = \flat$)

TO BOLDLY GO

By MICHAEL GIACCHINO
Contains portions of the TV Theme
by Alexander Courage and Gene Roddenberry